SCOTLAND
A Year of the Land

First English edition published by Colour Library Books
© 1983 Illustrations and Text: Colour Library International Ltd.
  99 Park Avenue, New York, N.Y. 10016, U.S.A.
This edition is published by Crescent Books
Distributed by Crown Publishers, Inc.
h g f e d c b a
Colour separations by FER-CROM, Barcelona, Spain.
Display and text filmsetting by ACESETTERS LTD., Richmond, Surrey, England.
Printed and bound in Barcelona, Spain by CAYFOSA and EUROBINDER
ISBN 0-517-414848
CRESCENT 1983

SCOTLAND
A Year of the Land

Text by IAN DIGBY

Produced by
TED SMART and DAVID GIBBON

CRESCENT BOOKS

Scotland and Greece, according to one travel authority, "are the two most romantic small countries in the world; both rich in scenery and history, both lavishly endowed with enchanting islands. But Greece," he complains, "is handicapped at times by too much sun, and Scotland by too much rain."

It is true that Scotland, particularly down the western side, is known for its rain, but then without a regular dousing the country just would not be Scotland. The heather and the bracken would not be the same, the burns that twinkle through the glen would perhaps not have quite the same sparkle and the national tipple – whisky – just might lack the refinement that has made it a favourite around the world.

But between the soft summer showers, that themselves can lend an invigoration and enchantment to a morning walk or an evening cruise, come those unforgettable days of clear skies when the traveller is tempted to lie low like the deer, grouse and ptarmigan, when little moves in the country except the buzzards wheeling round and round high above the glens. Then Scotland truly has so much to offer.

The country itself is dominated by its coastline and its islands – nearly 800 of them. The mainland at its longest measures no more than 280 miles, at its widest 150. The coastline runs to thousands of miles and it is said that much of Scotland in its noblest and loveliest aspects is viewable only from the deck of a ship; no-one, said the old Scottish writer J.J. Bell, should say he has seen a country with a coastline when he has toured it only from within. Today it is possible to see much of the coastal scenery from both sides, as it were.

Of those 800 islands, comprising Orkney, Shetland, the Firth of Clyde, the Firth of Forth, and the Inner and Outer Hebrides, only 60 or so are bigger than three square miles and most are uninhabited for geographical or economic reasons.

The mainland is divided into two parts – the Highlands and Lowlands. The Highlands are cleft by the Caledonian Canal, which links three lovely lochs and stretches some 60 miles from Fort William to Inverness. The Highlands also have a fertile tract of farming land lying between their foothills and the sea, running from Sutherland in the north down to the rich dairy country of Aberdeen and Kincardine in the east.

The Lowlands are perhaps dominated by the industrial belt that lies between Edinburgh and Glasgow where lives the bulk of the country's population. But there are also the dairy farms of Dumfries, Galloway and Ayrshire, the coal mining districts of Lanark and Fife and the sheep country on the borders in Roxburgh, Peebles and Berwick.

The distinction between Highlands and Lowlands is partly a geographical one. The hills and mountains to the north – Highland country – are bigger, more dramatic; but the main reason for the division is historical. It was to the north and west of the Highland line – roughly running from the northwest corner of Caithness to the south west border with England around the Firth of Clyde – that the Gaelic-speaking Celts retreated as the Kingdom of Scotland established itself. The Celts were not city dwellers; they lived in extended communities or clans, united by family ties and loyalty to their chiefs. They lived by cattle droving, hunting and, later, crofting and sea fishing.

So there is a cultural difference between the two Scotlands as well as a geographic one. But these days it is perhaps the difference in terrain that is most noticeable to the visitor. The hills and rivers of the Lowlands are less spectacular than their rockier equivalents to the north; the Lowlands have no such rugged peaks, and the grouse and deer moors of the Highlands are unknown south of the line.

Then there are the Islands. The first one the traveller from the south will encounter is Bass Rock, which looms out of the sea just to the north of the London-Edinburgh road. It is one of the ten Forth Islands, looked upon by the inhabitants of Edinburgh as their own. Glaswegians think similarly about the seven Firth of Clyde islands that include the well known and loved Arran, Bute and Ailsa Craig.

To the west lie the Hebrides, rich in legend and history, commemorated in song and orchestral music. The Inner Hebrides, the larger grouping of islands, include Skye with its Bonnie Prince Charlie connections, and Iona where St Columba landed in AD 563 to convert the heathen to Christianity. Other islands in the group, all of them with a ring to their names, include Mull, Jura, Islay, Rum, Eigg, Tyree and Colonsay.

Further out into the Atlantic lie the Outer Hebrides, flatter, more open it seems to the elements, where life is more rugged and hard-earned. Here are Lewis and Harris, the Uists, Eriskay, Barra and Benbecula.

The northern islands, where at midnight in midsummer it gets no darker than twilight, attractively called by the islanders "simmer dim," are divided between Orkney and Shetland. About half the 49 Orkneys are inhabited, largely by farmers and their families. According to Moray McLaren in his introduction to the Shell Guide to Scotland (Ebury Press, 1972), "the Orcadian is said to be a farmer who has a boat, while the Shetlander is a sailor and fisherman who has a croft or small piece of land on the side."

Shetlanders, who live on some 20 of the 117 islands in the group, are directly descended from the old Norsemen; they look Scandinavian, and their capital, Lerwick, bears little resemblance to any mainland town – Scottish or English – which is perhaps not surprising because the nearest city of any size is Bergen in Norway.

The Scots are farmers, coalminers, scholars, lawyers, engineers, golfers, footballers, shipbuilders and fishermen, although the last two industries have suffered grievously in recent years from recession and political interference. Some are thrifty, some so extravagant that, to use the vernacular of Fred Urquhart (*Scotland*, Batsford 1961), "they gaily throw their bonnets over the windmill." He describes his fellow countrymen as "proud, ambitious, passionate and parsimonious; cautious, reckless, solemn and gregarious. They have been – and still are – bonny fighters, and they have been great emigrants."

Novelist Alastair MacLean notes the same tendency to leave the "auld country." Writing in 1972 (*Scotland*, Deutsch) he attributed the exodus to the fact that Scots "are born adventurers. To the disgruntlement of large numbers of people, they are to be found virtually everywhere." Perhaps as many as 20 million are scattered around the world where, said MacLean, "they immediately set about forming a St Andrews Society and, inevitably, a Burns Society." The latter, he went on, "are allegedly dedicated to the preservation and honouring of the immortal bard, but for the majority of people at such gatherings Burns is synonymous not with poetry but with haggis and an endless river of Scotch." And at times like these, Maclean said, the classic dilemma of the wandering Scot is exposed. Obliged, for whatever reason to live and work abroad, the expatriate Scot believes there is no better place to live or die than his homeland, which he defends against allcomers with a deathless devotion.

Perhaps a clue to this innate urge to wander lies somewhere in Scotland's romantic and bloody history. It begins, as far as is known, about 6,000 years ago. The first inhabitants were probably descendants of people of the old Stone Age and were called the "Harpoon People" because harpoons made of deerhorn have been found among prehistoric remains. Similar remains have been found in Denmark dating from the time when Britain was still joined to continental Europe.

Subsequent immigrants came from the Mediterranean, from people descended from Central Asian tribes, from the Gaelic-speaking Celts and, just before the birth of Christ, from Britons with their knowledge of iron working. Then came the Romans, although never in their 300-year occupation did they master Scotland as they did England.

There is no city or town in Scotland whose founding can be traced to the Romans, nor are there any place names in the country, except possibly one or two in the Borders, which can truly be said to be of Roman origin. But the Romans did influence Scottish history by concentrating the different Pictish tribes who opposed them into defensive alliances which provided the cornerstone for the establishment of the nation when it came some centuries later.

But before that were to come other invaders, each of whom contributed in their own ways to Scotland and the Scots as we know them today. The Picts were established in the north and north-east of the country, then came the Scots from Northern Ireland to settle in the southern Hebrides before filtering inland; the Britons congregated in the Lowlands and the Angles occupied the south and south-west.

But then came the Norsemen, English fleeing the Norman conquest, Normans themselves and, later, with the opening up of trade, the Flemings.

Christianity had arrived in the sixth century with St Columba; although the Romans had brought a version of it with them, it never became established. By contrast, Ireland, which the Romans never occupied, was rapidly emerging as a leading Christian centre with the founding and subsequent development of many monasteries; from one such came Columba to settle on Iona, the result so one story goes of his copying a manuscript without permission, and being banished for his efforts.

For more than 30 years until his death in 597, St Columba spread the gospel, only for his work to be largely undone with the arrival of the Vikings, whose campaign of pillage and terror plunged Scotland into its own Dark Age which lasted until the arrival of the Normans in the south of England, and the establishment, with Malcolm Canmore, of a Scottish monarchy.

For nearly 200 years from that time the Scots were continually occupied in defending their territory against the English and the Scandinavians, but by 1265 Alexander III had taken the Hebrides and had removed Norway from all her possessions except Orkney and Shetland.

But with Alexander's death and no unchallenged heir, the Scottish future was again plunged into crisis, with the English under Edward I sensing an opportunity to bring the Scots under the English crown. Edward took his army north of the border and devastated the Scottish forces, bringing back with him – an act for which the Scots have never forgiven the English – the Stone of Scone on which Scottish kings had been crowned. The Stone has never officially been returned to Scotland since that time.

Under Robert the Bruce (more French than Scottish; his name was actually Robert de Brus), and after Edward's death in 1307, Scottish forces had more success, culminating in the inspirational victory at the Battle of Bannockburn seven years later, where they defeated the English who out-numbered them four to one.

But the Scots were unable to achieve any real political advantage from the victory and by the time they reached accord with the English, Scottish ties with France had been cemented to such an extent that any real friendship with England was out of the question.

The "Auld Alliance" between Scotland and France lasted for centuries and, because of it, Scots fought beside Joan of Arc, enlisted with the French in the Hundred Years War against England and, like the Stuarts, sought refuge in France from English oppression. It used to be said, "He that will France win, must with Scotland first begin."

With the accession to the throne of Robert the Bruce's grandson, Robert the Steward, the ill-fated house of Stuart first appears in Scottish history. But under Robert, Scotland started to flourish and the fifteenth century was, on balance, a good time to be born a Scot. Trade and commerce grew, many monasteries were built and three universities estab-lished – St Andrews 1412, Glasgow 1451 and Aberdeen 1495.

James IV had come to the throne in 1488 and under him life was never dull. He was very much a Renaissance man, speaking several European languages as well as Gaelic and Scots. He was ardent in almost everything he did – in religion, romance, public life, and battle. And he was highly popular. His attitude of mind, his proud spirit, his patronage of the arts created an intellectual and artistic climate in Scotland that produced much fine poetry and literature.

As important perhaps for the security of his people was his marriage to Henry VIII's sister, Margaret. But James was too volatile and impetuous for that to ensure peace. He quarreled with Henry and, while the English king was away fighting in France, James crossed the border with his army to invade England. It was a foolhardy enterprise, leading to the annihi-lation of the Scottish Army at Flodden and to James' death.

His son, James V, inherited the throne, in Stuart tradition, as a minor. He was in fact one-year-old. He also inherited a dilemma: Scotland could not remain neutral in the contin-uing Anglo-French conflict. She would have to ally herself with one or the other and take the inevitable consequences. The choice could not have been easy. On the one hand, James was a catholic and France was catholic, and the English were the old enemy; on the other hand, his mother was English and was the sister of the English king.

He chose France, married two French wives and fathered the tragic Mary Queen of Scots. While her mother, Mary of Guise, ruled as Regent of Scotland Mary spent much of her childhood in France, later marrying the French Dauphin. In 1561, a widow, she returned to govern Scotland, one year after the Scottish parliament, influenced by John Knox, had denounced Catholicism and established Protestantism.

As a Catholic Queen, she demanded the right to practise her own religion, while guaranteeing religious freedom to her people. She married twice – Darnley, who was murdered, and then, in an act which angered even her supporters, Bothwell, who was widely believed to be one of the assassins. He was a divorced Protestant and the marriage was a Protestant ceremony taking place with indecent haste after Darnley's death. Mary was condemned by everyone, including the Pope, was imprisoned, escaped, abdicated and fled to London, throwing herself on the mercy of Elizabeth, was again imprisoned and, 19 years later, executed.

It was much simpler for her son by Darnley. He was, like Mary had been, the legitimate heir to the English throne as well as the Scottish one, but he was a protestant and on Elizabeth's death in 1603 he became James I of England and James VI of Scotland, uniting the two kingdoms for the first time.

In the meantime John Knox had been motivating the Scottish Reformation, establishing the Scottish Reformed Kirk which, by the time James inherited the English Crown, was in dispute with the Church of England, although both were protestant faiths.

Before he left for London, James tried to soften the Kirk's attitude towards the English protestants but only succeeded in hardening it when, as head of the Church, he tried to insist on English-style services and hymnals in Scottish churches.

The result was deadlock, but before the dispute could be resolved, the English Civil War broke out. The wily Scots struck a bargain with Cromwell: they would fight for him at Marston Moor against the Royalists if he would grant them their Covenants – guarantees of their right to worship as they wished. The battle was won, the Covenants granted; but then Cromwell pushed the Scots too far: he beheaded Charles I. The Scots reacted by crowning his Catholic son, Charles II, on condition that he too would guarantee the

Covenants. Cromwell invaded Scotland and until the end of the Commonwealth in 1660 the country was subjugated. But with Charles II restored to both English and Scottish thrones, there began a persecution of the Covenanters which, along with many other religious disputes, was not resolved until the Act of Union in 1707 which established Scotland and England as one nation with one parliament, established Protestantism as the national religion, and ended forever any real possibility of a Catholic Stuart's accession to the throne.

After the Union, Moray McLaren wrote, "as individuals we Scots have richly benefited – there have been several Scottish prime ministers at Westminster and, even more impressive, at least two Scottish archbishops of Canterbury – but as a nation we have sadly lost. Inevitably as the smaller partner we have declined in identity while England, during the long period of prosperity before her, gained."

And if the Scottish Kirk thought its future was guaranteed it had to think again. Within five years the parliament at Westminster passed an act that effectively denied the right of Scottish congregations to elect their own minister. Instead they had to accept the choice of the local landowner, whether or not he was interested in the congregation or church matters. This act was at the root of many Scottish religious problems throughout the 18th century and was not truly resolved for some 140 years.

The Stuarts, too, made further attempts to rewrite the Act of Union. James Stuart's was never going to succeed in 1715 but his eldest son, Charles Edward – Bonnie Prince Charlie – was much more determined in 1745.

Virtually unaccompanied, he landed from France on Eriskay in the Hebrides and made his way inland, gathering support as he went. Among it – and proving decisive among fellow Scots – was that of Cameron of Lochiel, a highly regarded chief, who joined the prince with the rest of his clan. Charles unfurled the Jacobite standard at Glenfinnan and marched south. The famous '45 had begun.

He took Perth and Edinburgh and, after defeating an Anglo-German force at Prestonpans, the south of Scotland was once again in Stuart hands. He pressed on as far as Derby but was then advised to withdraw back to Scotland where he was later decisively beaten at Culloden by the Duke of Cumberland, whose atrocities and barbarous acts on the Scots earned him the nickname, "Butcher," and assured a permanent place in Scottish history for Culloden.

Charles escaped and despite a price of £30,000 offered for his capture – a huge sum in those days – none of his countrymen could be persuaded to betray him. He reached the Continent and died in Rome 43 years later.

The '45 led to the vicious repression of the Highlands and the clans. The Highlanders were disarmed, Highland dress was outlawed, the Gaelic tongue was proscribed and the land itself – the livelihood for thousands – was cleared of the crofts and converted to sheep grazing and, later, sporting estates. The Highland Clearances which continued until the late 19th century radically reduced the population, and many of the highlanders fled overseas, never to return.

But the second half of the 18th century did see an explosion of literary and intellectual talent in Scotland, or at least in the south, centred on Edinburgh. At this time Adam Smith, Robbie Burns, James Boswell, Sir Walter Scott and the Adam Brothers were all contributing to the national heritage.

In the 19th century the Church took the first step towards solving the problems stimulated by the 1712 Act that gave the local landowner the right to appoint the kirk's minister. In 1843 about 450 ministers walked out of the national assembly of the Church of Scotland to form the Free Church of Scotland which, until 1929 when the two amalgamated, was supported and maintained by the people, and not by patronage.

Queen Victoria, too, played a part in the revival of Scottish national identity which started towards the end of the century with her love of things Scottish and her regular visits to Balmoral; this sense of national pride and identity continues today – something most visitors to Scotland never fail to notice.

Writer Moray McLaren highlighted another Scots' virtue when he wrote: "The visitor will recognise one quality that was noticed so enthusiastically just over four and a half centuries ago by de Ayala, the Spanish Ambassador to James IV, a quality that still remains. It is hospitality."

Religion is important to the Scots, although nowadays it is not practised with the fervour that led T.S. Eliot to remark, "Scotland is a country ruined by religion." He was talking about the strictly orthodox Calvinist reformed faith which took hold of the country in the 16th century under John Knox, and still exists – albeit in diluted form – throughout Presbyterian Scotland. However, pockets of orthodox concentration still survive, largely in the Islands and North West Highlands where the so-called "Wee Frees," still practise the religion as did the founding members of the Free Church of Scotland when it was set up in 1843.

In these areas nothing happens and little moves on the Sabbath. You cannot buy petrol, food, newspapers or even book into a hotel. Bed and Breakfast signs are covered up each Sunday, travel of any kind is avoided and diversions such as Highland Games or even Christmas dinner, when that falls on a Sunday, are strictly forbidden. But these are small communities and many tourists can drive through them without being aware of the Sunday stringencies.

The visitor to Scotland could be forgiven, as he drives through town after town, particularly in the Lowlands, for thinking that the Scots live almost exclusively on a diet of fish and chips. Certainly those two commodities are a staple ingredient of the Scottish diet but no-one should leave the country without trying some of the national dishes. Contrary to popular belief, haggis is not some wild beastie that roams the Highland moors. It is a tasty, spicy mixture of sheeps liver, heart, lights, oatmeal, onion, pepper, salt, nutmeg, stock and lemon, boiled inside a sheep's paunch and usually served with mashed potatoes and turnip. It is, perhaps, an acquired taste and there's no better place to acquire it than in its homeland.

Oatcakes are also a must while in Scotland. They were originally made from the oats grown by crofters, ground, then baked over an open fire. When fresh and well made, spread with a little butter, they are delicious. The best advice is to shop around and to buy daily.

And then, of course, there's porridge. Many English people have childhood memories of trying to force the stuff down at breakfast, while a bearded, kilted, caber-tossing figure of a Highlander looked on from the front of the porridge packet. The message undoubtedly was; eat your porridge and you too would grow up to be a strapping figure of a man. If made well, and not out of a packet, it certainly is an excellent way to start a day of hill trekking, early morning fishing, ski-ing or whatever. The purists eat it just with salt, but sugar and milk, treacle or butter are just as good and more palatable.

The Scottish kipper must also be tried, particularly if the herring has only recently been fished out of the sea or a loch. Loch Fyne kippers have a splendid reputation and, if you've time for a lingering breakfast, are delicious cooked in butter. On the Islands, you can even get them smoked over a peat fire and that really is the best way to smoke a herring.

Peat, while not being as widespread as in Ireland, is still widely cut in Scotland and is particularly noticeable on the Islands where the peat industry still flourishes. Peat is formed on land where the soil is too wet and cold to allow bacteria to break down the dead matter in the usual way. Rain washes much of the goodness out of the humus, making the soil increasingly acidic. It occurs on those areas where there is poor drainage and no blown sand to counteract the acidity. The Outer Hebrides provide ideal peat conditions.

Once dried, peat is a marvellous fuel. A few days' peat cutting can supply a year's requirements. The cutting is done in the spring when the peat is taken out in "bricks" and stacked flat on the heather for drying in the summer winds. In bad summers it never dries out and is just left to rot, but in most years by September the peat is dry enough to be carried back to the croft and stacked close to the house. It must be comforting to the crofters to know that when the world has run dry of oil, gas and coal, there will still be peat available to warm their homes.

Scotland's four main cities are Glasgow, the oldest, Edinburgh, Aberdeen and Dundee. Nearly two million of the country's five and a half million people live in them.

Glasgow, said H.V. Morton, "plays the part of Chicago to Edinburgh's Boston. Glasgow is a city of the glad hand and the smack on the back; Edinburgh is a city of silence until birth or brains open the social circle. In Glasgow a man is innocent until found guilty; in Edinburgh a man is guilty until he is found innocent. Glasgow is willing to believe the best of an unknown quantity; Edinburgh, like all aristocracies, the worst."

Those words were written nearly fifty years ago and Edinburgh's inhabitants might well now dispute them, but there is undoubtedly a gulf between the two; more perhaps of attitude than anything else. Glasgow is the practical, down-to-earth city, prepared to dirty its hands, build factories, surround itself with industry; Edinburgh strikes a loftier pose; more a city for the professional man, for the academic, for the arts.

But Glasgow was on the map before Edinburgh – founded around AD 500 when St Mungo built his chapel by a ford on the River Clyde, a site now occupied by the Cathedral, which is the only pre-Reformation Gothic structure still standing on the Scottish mainland. Its vaulted crypt is one of Europe's finest and the well, in which St Mungo is said to have performed baptisms, still attracts many visitors.

The best vantage point for a view of the cathedral is across the Bridge of Sighs in the Necropolis, the graveyard of the Merchants' House of Glasgow. It was opened in 1832, was modelled on the Père-la-Chaise cemetery in Paris, and presiding over it is a statue of John Knox.

The oldest house in Glasgow stands in Cathedral Square. Now a museum, Provand's Lordship was built in 1471 for the priest in charge of St Nicholas Hospital. Mary Queen of Scots is supposed to have lived in the house and while there to have written the famous "casket letters."

Jocelyn Square, below the Saltmarket, is worth a visit. On one side is Scotland's High Court, the Justiciary Buildings; on the other is Glasgow Green, said to be Britain's oldest public park, which contains the first monument ever erected to Lord Nelson (1806). Also on the Green are the Old Glasgow Museum and the Fleshers' Haugh, where Bonnie Prince Charlie reviewed his troops in 1745.

George Square, Glasgow's Trafalgar Square, is regarded as the centre of the city. Glasgow citizens traditionally celebrate national and international events there, such as a football victory over the English, the end of wars, and so on. A statue of Sir Walter Scott is one of twelve set in the square surrounded by company and municipal buildings. The City Chambers there, opened by Queen Victoria in 1888, were built inside and out in the grand Italian Renaissance style.

Buchanan, Argyle and Sauchiehall Streets are the main shopping areas. At the bottom of Sauchiehall Street is Kelvingrove with its impressive art galleries, Kelvin Hall, a big exhibition centre and the university, an impressive building designed by Sir George Gilbert Scott in the 1870s.

Glasgow's first museum, the Hunterian, is housed in the grounds of the university. Named after William Hunter, a doctor of medicine at the University, it exhibits among other things coins, prints and a collection of Whistler paintings.

Built upon hills, with higher peaks soaring behind it and the Firth of Forth at its feet, Edinburgh enjoys a dramatic location. From Arthur's seat, the highest point in the city, you can see half of Southern Scotland and, on a good day, as far as the Highlands.

Old Edinburgh probably dates back to the early seventh century, when King Edwin of Northumbria established a settlement around the Rock, possibly known as Edwin's burgh. But the city, although used as Scotland's capital by several monarchs in the 15th and 16th centuries, did not really establish itself until the Victorian era when the old and new town first truly came together.

There is so much to see in Edinburgh but you should really start with St Margaret's Chapel, perched high on Edinburgh Castle Rock. Margaret, Scottish queen and saint, had it built for worship in 1076. Measuring only sixteen feet by ten

within the nave, it is Edinburgh's oldest building and perhaps the oldest intact structure in Scotland. There, in her last days and with the castle under siege, she heard from her son, later King David I, that her husband and her eldest son had just died in battle.

The Castle itself, first mentioned as a royal residence in 1004, is not complete but highspots for the visitor are the royal apartments which Scottish monarchs used before union with England in 1707; where Mary Queen of Scots gave birth to her son, the future James I of England and VI of Scotland; the Crown Chamber containing the regalia of Scotland, including a gold circlet on the crown that Robert the Bruce may have worn; and the Great Hall which dates from 1424.

The Castle also has a custom you can set your watch by. At 1 p.m. every day since 1861 the cannon of the Half-Moon Battery has been fired – a custom borrowed from Paris.

From the Castle the famous Royal Mile stretches out past Castle Hill, into Lawnmarket, beside St Giles Cathedral where John Knox preached and into Canongate before ending at Holyroodhouse. It was at Holyrood that Mary's favourite, the Italian Rizzio, was murdered and you can still see the tiny room where the dastardly deed was done; it was at Holyrood where James VI first heard from a mud-bespattered messenger, weary from the ride from London, that Queen Elizabeth I was dead and that he was now also James I of England; and it was at Holyrood that Bonnie Prince Charlie, in 1745, first appeared before the people of Edinburgh.

Apart from the shopping prospects it offers, Princes Street also contains the Scottish National Gallery and the Royal Scottish Academy and, just by the Mound, built into the bed of Princes Street Gardens, a huge floral clock made up of some 20,000 plants with a "cuckoo" that appears every quarter hour.

In East Princes Street Gardens you can climb the 287 steps to the top of the 200-foot Scott monument for a fine view over the new part of the city.

Aberdeen, the Granite City – so called because much of it is built from granite mined locally at Rubislaw – lies between two rivers, the Dee and the Don, and looks out upon a broad bay. Like Edinburgh, the city is composed of the old and the new, blending together into vistas of broad streets and elegant buildings. It is a city of statues, among them King Edward VII, Robert Burns, Prince Albert and Sir William Wallace. St Machar's Cathedral is the only granite cathedral in Britain and is named after a disciple of Columba's who was sent from Iona to establish Christianity where Aberdeen now stands. Although declining, the fishing industry is still a presence in Aberdeen and the daily early morning fish market is a reminder of the city's heritage. But it is oil that now dominates the city's economy and the trappings of the industry – oil company offices, fleets of tankers, and new leisure and restaurant facilities – are visible on almost every street.

Scotland's third city, Dundee, with a population of about 200,000, dates back to Roman times, and the remains of old Roman camps can still be seen in the surrounding countryside. The city's most ancient landmark is the Old Steeple in the Nethergate which is actually a massive battlemented square tower, 156 feet high, containing a beautiful little hall, with a lofty, groined roof and some finely carved figures. The River Tay sweeps past the city, a reminder of the 1879 Tay Bridge disaster when the Edinburgh-Dundee train plunged through a gaping hole in the wind-torn structure.

A stormy history and mountainous terrain usually mean castles, and Scotland is no disappointment in that direction. Probably one of the most instantly recognisable – photographs of its dramatic setting have appeared widely – is Eilean Donan, near Dornie on the road to Skye, where Lochs Alsh, Long and Duich meet. Dating from the Middle Ages it was for long a stronghold of the Mackenzies of Kintail. So strong were its defences that in 1539 the castle was held by two men and a boy against a fleet of galleys. After some years in private ownership, the castle is now open to the public.

At least as famous is Dunvegan Castle on the Isle of Skye. The seat of the Macleod chiefs, it is the oldest castle continuously in the same family ownership. Its foundations may contain stones of a fort that stood on the rock a thousand years ago, though the oldest part of the castle itself dates from the 13th century. One of the bloodiest episodes in its history was the day in 1552 when eleven Campbells of Argyll were invited to a banquet where each was placed between two Macleods. The feast over, a cup was placed in front of each Campbell, and filled with blood. This was the signal for the Macleods to draw their dirks and slaughter their guests. Among the relics on public view at the castle are the two-handed sword that belonged to Rory Mor, the clan's 12th chief, and a "fairy flag" believed to have been captured from the Saracens during the Wars of the Crusades.

Inverary Castle on the shores of Loch Fyne was originally built in the 15th century by Campbell of Glenurchy and for more than 400 years it has been the residence of successive earls, marquises and dukes of Argyll. The present building was erected in 1745, restored in 1879-80, and is an impressive early example of the neo-Gothic style in Britain.

Balmoral Castle is the private holiday home of Queen Elizabeth. Prince Albert bought it and the grounds in 1852 and had it re-modelled, using granite quarried from the 24,000-acre Balmoral Estate. Built in the Scottish baronial style, it consists of two separate blocks of buildings connected by wings, with a massive tower at one angle measuring 35 feet square and 80 feet high. On top is a turret with circular staircase pushing the total height to 100 feet.

Craigievar Castle, 25 miles west of Aberdeen, has to be seen to be believed. It is not only everyman's idea of the traditional fairytale castle, it is an architectural gem as well, described by one historian as claiming "a Scottish place in the front rank of European architecture." Now owned by the Scottish National Trust, it was built in 1626 and has been little changed since that time. It was in the care of the Forbes family till the Trust took over; a family whose motto "Do not vaiken sleiping dogs" can still be seen on the arch of the main stairway. Other features of the castle are the Queen's bedroom, with its canopied bed and decorated ceiling, and the Blue Room lighted by the windows of the turrets.

Overlooking Loch Ness, Urquhart Castle has been a ruin for nearly 300 years; much of what now remains dates from 1509. It has two unopened vaults, one of which is said to contain treasure, the other; plague-infested clothing. No-one knows which is which and, not surprisingly, no-one is keen to find out.

Near Golspie is Dunrobin Castle, seat of the Dukes of Sutherland. This "Gothic mistake, all minarets and turrets," as one critic called it, is largely 19th century. Part of the castle is open as a museum for objêts and mementos collected by various members of the family and for stuffed wildlife exhibits such as otter, wildcat, marten, badger, fox and stoat.

Also worth a visit, among Scotland's many castles, is the Castle of Mey overlooking the Pentland Firth on the north coast of the Scottish mainland. Now the home of the Queen Mother, it was built in 1556 and inherited by the Sinclairs of Mey who left it in 1889 after 300 years of occupation. It was under threat of demolition when the Queen Mother bought it in 1952.

Another home that attracts many visitors on pilgrimage each year is that of Sir Walter Scott, at Abbotsford near Melrose. Scott, the author of *Ivanhoe, Kenilworth* and *Rob Roy*, bought it in 1812 and lived there until his death in 1832. Abbotsford, for his last six years there, must have seemed almost a prison. In 1826 his business partners left him with an enormous debt of £117,000, which Scott decided to pay off through earnings from his books. In those six years he worked furiously to pay off the debt, earning £80,000. But he wrote himself into the grave. Scott built Abbotsford in instalments. It is a many-turreted mansion standing among trees and built on rising ground which slopes gently to the River Tweed. Much of the inside of the house has been preserved in the state in which Scott himself knew it.

Scotland's other great writer, Robbie Burns, coming from humbler origins, has a humbler memorial. His cottage lies in Alloway just outside Ayr. Built in 1758, the year before Burns was born, the cottage is the oldest building in the town and in its grounds is a fine museum of manuscripts and other relics. The area is full of Burns references. In Ayr there is the Tam O' Shanter Inn, the Auld Brid and the New Bridge. In Alloway there is the charming Brig o' Doon and the "auld haunted kirk." In Dumfries there are two taverns in which he drank – the Globe and the Hole in the Wa'. At nearby Lincluden Burns saw his "Vision of Libertie" and composed "Mary in Heaven" while staying at Ellisland Farm.

Scotland is also lochs and glens, rivers and waterfalls, mountains and peaks. Loch Katrine in the Trossachs is one loch of the many that have been immortalised in verse at one time or another. Scott wrote, "One burnished sheet of living gold, Loch Katrine lay beneath him rolled." And Dorothy Wordsworth, describing a sail on the loch wrote, "It was an entire solitude; and all that we beheld was the perfection of loveliness and beauty." On its shores are the so-called Royal Cottage where Queen Victoria stopped to rest in 1859 and up towards the end of the two-mile loch, near Glengyle, is a house with an odd window in the thick wall of the sitting room. Rob Roy is said to have used it as a loophole for his musket.

Before the River Dochart tumbles into the waters of Loch Tay near Killin in Perthshire at the Falls of Dochart, it flows round a dark, rocky islet – the ancient burial grounds of the Clan Macnab. It is a sombre spot even on a sunny day. Nearby are Kinnell House, one time home of the clan chiefs, and the ruins of Finlarig Castle built in 1523 by Black Duncan of the Cowl. From the bridge over the river there is a view of the wide valley of the Dochart and, on a clear day, of Ben More's 3,843 feet.

Loch Maree in Ross and Cromarty is rich in legend. Eighteen miles long and once joined to Loch Ewe, the sea loch, its surface is dotted by more than 20 small, wooded islands. On one of them, Eilean Maree, are the remains of a monastery, said to have been founded by St Maree from Iona, and the graves of a Norse prince and princess. It also contains a holy well to which the insane were once brought to be cured.

Perhaps the most famous of Scottish Lochs, along with Ness, is Loch Lomond. At 24 miles long and varying between one and five miles wide it is the largest expanse of inland water in Great Britain. It has some 30 wooded islands, the largest of which is Inchmurrin. Inchcaillach, or the "women's island," has the ruins of a nunnery and is the burial place of the MacGregors. Tobias Smollett, surgeon turned novelist, wrote of it: "I have seen the Lago di Garda, Albano di Vico, Bolsena and Geneva, and I prefer Loch Lomond to them all . . . Everything there is romantic beyond imagination." From Rowardennan on the east bank, you can make the long, but not difficult, walk to the top of Ben Lomond, 3,192 feet up, for some spectacular views.

Loch Ness is in the Great Glen, about seven miles from Inverness. It is as long as Lomond but not as wide, although at 700 feet it is considerably deeper. It also has an unrivalled legend that has been intriguing the world ever since 1932 when it first hit the headlines, and intriguing locals since as long ago as the seventh century. It was also used for an attempt on the world water speed record by John Cobb in 1952. The attempt ended tragically in his death and a cairn in his memory stands on the western shore between Drumnadrochit and Invermoriston.

Loch Awe in Argyll rivals Lomond for natural beauty. Dominated by the towering peak of Ben Cruachan, it provides excellent salmon and trout fishing where once the Campbell clan ruled unrivalled. Many of the islands have ruins of old castles or fortifications from the days when the Campbells used the Loch almost as a moat for their huge territory stretching all around Inverary.

Loch Leven, only 12 miles or so from Dunfermline, is where St Serf gave his name to the largest island, which bears the ruins of his ninth century priory. On the smaller Castle Island still stands the tower of the castle in which Mary Queen of Scots was made to sign the Deed of Abdication. In 1568, with the help of friends, she escaped by boat from the isle, locking her guards inside the castle and dropping the keys into the Loch. In 1805 those same keys were found among the rushes on the Lochside and can now be seen at the Scott home of Abbotsford. Within days of the escape Mary suffered her final defeat in the Battle of Langside, near Glasgow, and fled south.

Of Scotland's many dramatic and beautiful glens, Glen Coe with its brooding atmosphere and bloody history is the most famous. Many writers have captured the foreboding they found in the Glen, none more so perhaps than Dickens. It had, he wrote, "the aspect of a burial place of a race of giants . . . Anything so bleak and wild and mighty in its loneliness is impossible to conceive. The pass is an awful place, shut in on each side by enormous rocks from which great torrents come rushing down in all directions. There are scores of glens high up which form such haunts as you might imagine yourself wandering in in the very height and madness of a fever ... The very recollection of them makes me shudder."

Seven-and-a-half miles long, the Glen runs from the desolate Rannoch Moor to the shores of Loch Leven. High up one of its hills, Aonach Dubh, is Ossian's Cave, which can be reached by climbing Ossian's Ladder, a moderately difficult rock climb. Ossian was a third century Gaelic bard and legend has it that he was born in the cave – a more uncomfortable birth place cannot be imagined.

Most visitors to the Glen come to see the site of the Massacre which took place in 1692. The previous year all the chiefs in the area, many of whom still supported the Stuarts, were asked to take an oath of allegiance to King William in London. They were threatened with "the utmost extremity of law" if they failed to do so by the end of 1691.

By the end of that year all had done so except Macdonald of Glengarry and MacIan of Glen Coe. In early January 1692 MacIan finally took the oath but in London it was either ignored or arrived too late and orders were issued to Campbell of Glen Lyon to make an example of MacIan and the Macdonalds who lived in Glen Coe. For twelve days Campbell, with 120 men, lived among the unsuspecting Macdonalds. Then, on the night of 13 February, the soldiers fell upon their hosts, killing some 40 of them and leaving others to die in the hills above, where they had fled. The Macdonald monument stands in the strath near the old road to Invercoe. MacIan is buried on Eilean Munde island in Loch Leven near the entrance to the Glen.

Almost due east of Glen Coe lies the Pass of Killiecrankie near Pitlochry. Through this beautiful gorge, now a Scottish National Trust beauty spot, runs the River Garry which, in its course of 22 miles, descends 1,000 feet. For nearly two miles along its banks runs an attractive riverside walk. In the Pass the Jacobites gained one of their few victories against William III and the Soldier's Leap is a formidable jump said to have been achieved by one of the fleeing soldiers of the beaten General Mackay's army.

Glen Garry is exquisite. Beyond the still, blue loch the river flows with Highland grace through a valley green with birch trees. Dark clumps of nettles mark the ruins of old crofts – the remains of houses burned down or left to rot during the Highland Clearances. Colonel Alastair MacDonell, a Glengarry, was the last Highland chief to travel the country with a band of retainers, known as Glengarry's Tail. "He

seemed," wrote H.V. Morton, "quite unconscious of a changed age and lived, dressed and behaved as if he existed in the Highlands of the 16th century." He died in 1828 when a steamer in which he was travelling foundered off the coast near Fort William. After his death huge debts forced the family abroad and today many of the Macdonald descendants from those times can be found in Glengarry, Ontario.

Glenfinnan is a national landmark for all Scots. Apart from its beauty – it is where the Road to the Isles passes the head of Loch Shiel – this is the spot where the standard of Bonnie Prince Charlie was raised on 19 August 1745 as a rallying point for the clans at the start of the great '45. The monument there was erected in 1815 by Macdonald of Glenaladale, grandson of one of the chiefs who was there on that August day.

The longest glen in Scotland is Glen Lyon. The entrance to it is dramatic. The sides of the glen rise steeply and are heavily wooded and down where the river flows in a deep rocky bed is Macgregor's Leap, where yet another clansman escaped his pursuers. Near the head of the glen, Meggernie Castle, dating from the 16th century, punctures the skyline. At the eastern end of the glen lies Fortingall, a village of light brown cottages roofed with dark brown thatch. Here, the story goes, Rome sent emissaries who were received by King Metellanus. One of them became the father of a son who was to grow up bearing one of the most infamous names in history – Pontius Pilate.

King of the Scottish peaks – and the highest in Great Britain – is Ben Nevis at 4,418 feet. Yet the first sight for many people is disappointing. Because its summit does not rise to a sharp peak, and because there are two other mountains within a mile of Nevis, it lacks the majesty of a king. There is a safe route to the top by bridle track from Achintee in Glen Nevis but the round trip of 10 miles usually takes eight to ten hours. The climber's route is the north-east face, which can be seen to its best effect from Corpach near Fort William.

Ben Cruachan is a collection of seven or eight peaks, the highest of which towers nearly 3,700 feet. Its lower slopes are wooded, its upper bare and lumpy, and its top is split into two cones. Its name is also the war cry of Clan Campbell.

Scotland's second highest peak, at 4,296 feet, is Ben Macdhui. It rises from the Cairngorms, where there are several other peaks of more than 4,000 feet, and provides excellent ski-ing in the winter.

And so to the Islands, starting with those of the Forth, where perhaps the best known and most instantly recognisable is

The Bass Rock. It is a haven for seabirds, among them gannets, fulmars, kittiwakes and razorbills; and seals can also be seen there, basking on the rocks in good weather. It is no longer inhabited, rises 350 feet from the sea and has through its centre a tunnel 170 yards long that can be explored at low tide. The biggest of the Forth Islands is May, which has been for more than 25 years a national nature reserve, equipped with facilities for observing the bird life and plant communities. Cramond is the only island in the group offering easy access. At low tide you can walk to it. Until the 19th century it was inhabited, the last occupant being a herdsman, the remains of whose dwelling still stand. He made a fortune from the oyster beds around the island, now sadly polluted.

Glasgow's islands, as they are called – the Islands of the Clyde – are: Bute, Arran, Ailsa Craig and Great Cumbrae. Bute calls itself the Madeira of Scotland and the municipal gardens at Ardencraig with its subtropical vegetation and cockatoos and canaries go some way towards justifying the claim. Bute was occupied centuries ago by many early monastics and evidence of their cells can be found all over the island. St Blane's Chapel on its hilltop site is one of the best-preserved Celtic monastic sites in Britain, dating back to the sixth century. There are also iron age forts to be seen, the most impressive of which is Dunnalant.

Arran, 55 miles round on the coastal road, has mountain scenery in the hinterland to rival the Highlands and holiday resort areas all around the coast. The highest peak is Goat Fell where, nearly a hundred years ago, a celebrated murder took place. One of the island's best viewpoints is Kingscross Point, so named because here Robert the Bruce watched the Ayrshire coast across the water for a sign from his supporters that they were ready to welcome him. He saw what he thought was the pre-arranged signal and set sail, only to find it was a false alarm.

Skye, of the Inner Hebrides, is the largest of the Western Isles, nearly 50 miles long and 23 across. Mountainous, with two chief ranges, the Cuillins and the Trotternish ridge, Skye had much Norse history, as its place names indicated, before joining the Kingdom of Scotland after the Norsemen's defeat at Largs in 1263. Since then the ruling family has been the Macleods of Dunvegan. It was to Skye that Flora Macdonald took Bonnie Prince Charlie, disguised as her maidservant, after his defeat. Flora was married in Skye and is now buried there, at Kilmuir.

Mull has the dubious reputation of being the wettest of the Hebridean islands, but visitors should not let that deter them. The chief town, Tobermory, is a port for the steamers and local yachtsmen and its 19th century houses are brightly painted in colours reminiscent of an Italian or Spanish fishing village. Among the scenic delights are countless waterfalls, the basalt cliffs around Ben More, the granite quarries of the Ross of Mull, whose stone was used in London's Albert Memorial, and the basalt columns of Ulva and Carsaig.

MacKinnon's Cave on the island has never been explored to its full extent. The story goes that MacKinnon, one of Scotland's legendary pipers, was exploring the cave when the tide started to come into it. A wicked fairy promised he would be saved if he could play the pipes until daylight. He failed and perished. The gloomy Glen More plays a part in Stevenson's *Kidnapped*, fully described as the hero, David Balfour, makes his way to the ferry at Craignure.

Staffa is famous for its Fingal's Cave, named after Ossian's father, and celebrated by Mendelssohn in his hugely popular Hebridean Overture, written after his visit in 1829.

Iona has been called the Cradle of the Celtic Kingdom of Scotland, established when St Columba arrived from Ireland in AD 563. An Abbey was built and successfully defended by the monks against the Viking invasions. The settlement only fell into disrepair at the time of the Scottish Reformation in the 16th century. It has now been revived with the foundation of a modern community of church people and craftsmen who have repaired the Abbey and recreated the community to meet the needs of the 20th century. Many kings are buried there from Ireland, Scotland and, it is believed, France and Norway, too. The first Celtic King of Scotland, Kenneth MacAlpine, is certainly buried there.

The remains of the old monastery, the conventual buildings, the burial places of the kings as well as the restored abbey all lie within easy reach of the landing stage for the ferry.

Colonsay (Columba's Isle) is littered with archaeological sites – standing stones, duns, circles and hill forts. It is also a walker's delight. Nowhere is restricted, not even the gardens of Colonsay House, owned by Lord Strathcona, which are ripe with magnolias, rhododendrons, peaches and figs.

Whisky and cheese occupy most of the inhabitants of Islay – making it, not consuming it. There are eight distilleries on the island. But once it had a far more significant role in the tide of Scottish history, for here was the seat of the Lords of the Isles. The Macdonald clan was founded here in the 12th century and for the next 300 years the Isles were ruled from Islay.

Lewis is the largest and most northerly of the Outer Hebrides, and is the home and stronghold of Gaelic – both language and culture. Fishing is the major industry, along with crofting, weaving and peat digging. Near the harbour of the chief town, Stornoway, is the Castle of Lewis, seat of the MacLeods of Lewis, owners from the 13th century until the island was granted to the Seaforth family by James V. After the First World War, ownership moved to soap millionaire Lord Leverhulme who, after attempting to market the island's products worldwide, gave the castle and the parish to its inhabitants. The area is now managed by the Stornoway Trust.

About six miles from Stornoway is St Columba's Chapel, founded by a MacLeod of Lewis for Augustinian canons. The seventh Macleod, Roderick, is buried there.

Benbecula is a fisherman's paradise, with many small inland lochs teeming with trout. The island links the strongly protestant and largely Free Kirk Northern Hebrides with the Catholic southern islands. In the old days the catholics, not having a church of their own on the island, had to ford the narrow sea crossing to South Uist for their religious services.

Flora Macdonald was born on South Uist; a cairn marks the spot in Miltons, surrounded by the remnants of the cottage. But she lived most of her time on Skye, apart from a brief sojourn in America.

Eriskay is formed by two bare and knobbly hill peaks, Ben Scrien and Ben Stack. Prince's Bay marks the spot where Bonnie Prince Charlie first set foot on Scottish soil at the beginning of the 1745 uprising. The sea bindweed that grows on the island is said by locals to have been brought by the Prince and is called the Prince's Flower. The island has also seen its share of wrecks, one such, the SS Politician, which ran aground carrying whisky, provided Sir Compton Mackenzie with the inspiration for his best-selling book, and later film, *Whisky Galore.*

The islands of Orkney are rich in archaeological interest. They contain a world famous Neolithic village, the oldest house in Europe still standing, Viking longhouses, duns, brochs and standing stones.

Kirkwall, on Orkney itself, was established by Norsemen in the 11th century, from which time dates the impressive St Magnus Cathedral in the town. The ruins of the Bishops Palace, built by Bishop William the Old, are next to the cathedral. King Haakon of Norway died there after his defeat at the Battle of Largs. Opposite the cathedral is the Tankerness Museum, showing much of Orkney history over the past 4,000 years.

On the road south from Kirkwall fine views can be obtained over Scapa Flow and on calm days you can actually make out, below the surface of the sea, the outline of the Royal Oak, torpedoed by a German submarine during the Second World War with the loss of 800 lives. It is a designated National War Grave.

Stromness, Orkney's second town, was developed by the Hudson's Bay Company in the 17th century and at one time three-quarters of the company's employees were Orcadians. North of the town is Scara Brae, the remains of a village built 4,500 years ago by a community of about 30 Stone Age people. Preserved by encroaching sand, the village is in extraordinarily good condition. Stone beds and dressers, cupboards and querns are exactly as they were when abandoned about 2450 BC.

Papa Westray has the oldest standing house in Europe – the Knap of Howar, meaning knob of the mounds. The two adjacent houses face Westray across the water and have been dated by scientists to somewhere between 3500 and 3100 BC. The island also has a bird reserve centred on the cliffs of Fowl's Craig, the last European breeding site of the now extinct Great Auk. Shag, tern, kittiwake and guillemot now populate the cliffs.

Hoy is the most westerly of the Orkney Islands, but is perhaps famous for another reason – the Old Man of Hoy; not an aged resident, but a vertical, 450-foot stack of old red sandstone, a challenge to every experienced rock climber.

Shetland lies 60 miles north of Orkney and consists of nearly 100 islands, of which about 20 are inhabited. Wool and knitted goods are what the islands are famous for. Lerwick is the capital and very much a focal point for fishermen from Denmark, Norway, Holland, Russia as well as the Shetlanders themselves. A Shetlander actually became prime minister of New Zealand – Robert Stout emigrated in 1863 and 21 years later was elected to office. He became Sir Robert.

Shetland, too, has its archaeological sites, the most famous being Jarlshof. The earliest remains on the site are of an oval hut dating from the Stone and early Bronze Age, some 3,000 years ago. Robert Louis Stevenson used Jarlshof in his story, *The Pirate;* he has another connection with the area – his grandfather built the lighthouse at Sumburgh Head.

Scalloway was once more important than Lerwick but now no longer even supports a shop. It is overlooked by the castle built by Andrew Crawford for the son of James V. The son, Patrick Stewart, has never been forgiven for imposing feudalism on the Islands and changing the traditional status of the islanders from freemen to bondmen.

Both the Shetland and Orkney Islands have been hugely affected by the North Sea oil and gas industries. Sullom Voe on Shetland was once a quiet bay where duck used to winter. Now it is covered by a vast oil terminal with pipelines from the Ninian and Brent oilfields beneath the sea pumping the oil into large tanks. It has brought wealth to the islands, but the cost to the environment has yet to be measured.

Sport and leisure have grown enormously in recent years as Scotland has looked more and more to tourism as a means of employment and a source of income.

Skiing attracts enthusiasts to several areas in the winter. Chief among them are Glencoe, Glen Shee, Lecht and the Spey Valley, including Aviemore in the Cairngorms. The main ski area at Aviemore is Coire Cas, where there are two chairlifts taking skiers up to 3,600 feet, seven tows and cafés and restaurants. Nearby Coire na Ciste boasts Britain's highest restaurant, situated at 3,750 feet.

Golf is a major sport in Scotland with its legendary St Andrews courses – 15 within easy reach of the town, including four in the town itself. The Old Course at St Andrews is said to go back to the 15th century. It was certainly played regularly in the 1700s before the Royal and Ancient Golf Club was founded in 1754. It has two of the most famous holes – the short 11th or "Sea" hole and the 17th, the "Road" hole, both of which have brought many of the world's

leading players down to earth with a bump. There is such demand to play at St Andrews – and anyone can do so – that on the Old Course who gets on the course and who does not is decided by ballot. Names must be in before 2.15 on the previous day and the lucky ones are then listed at the club, the Caddie's shelter, local golf clubs and the Information Centre in the town's South Street.

You can go board sailing, wind surfing if you like, at Lochearnhead and Loch Insh among many locations; canoeing at Loch Insh and Dulnain Bridge; fishing just about anywhere there's water; hang gliding near Braemar; mountaineering, hill walking, pony trekking, dinghy sailing, and even gold panning.

You can visit the splendid homes and gardens owned by Scotland's National Trust; you can watch Braemar's Highland Games, Highland Gatherings at Strathpeffer, Invergordon, Dornoch, Lochinver, Thurso, Dingwall, Strathconon and Durness among many. There are sea angling festivals, county shows, regattas, craft centres and potteries; in fact everyone is catered for.

Or you can just do what the majority of travellers to Scotland find so satisfying: drink-in the sheer beauty of the country; enjoy the hospitality of its inhabitants and give a resounding "yes" to the question posed by the old Scots song, "Will ye no come back again?"

'The Orkney Islands, mountains, capes, and heights,
And lengthened stretch of bay-indented coast,
Whose cliffs arise, a bold, defiant host,
From which the shattered might of ocean reels.'
GRANT

Assailed and battered by foam-flecked Atlantic breakers, the sea-cliffs of Scotland's West Coast and Orkney Isles *these pages* are among the most spectacular in the world. The whole scene is drenched by salt-spray and drowned in the continual pounding thunder of waves and the constant wail of screaming sea-birds.

The most magical and yet the most terrifying scenery in the British Isles – the Highlands of Scotland – are a land of awesome mountain ranges and wild sea lochs, of frowning crags and darkly shadowed passes, whose grandeur moved Scott to write of it '... a scene of natural beauty and romance; high hills, rocks and banks waving with natural forests of birch and oak as their leaves rustle to the wind and twinkle in the sun, gave to the depth of solitude a sort of life and vivacity.'

Remote and magnificently desolate stand the Heights of Scotland, whose torturous snow-capped summits are brought into perfect harmony, reflected in the blue waters of their lakes. Such visions are the hills of Black Mount on Rennoch Moor *above*, Loch Garry *left*, Loch Leven at Ballachullish *top left* and the River Beathach at Glen Orchy *right*, whose –

'... wild solitudes, lengthen'd and deep,
where the sheep's bleat or that rare sound,
the harsh scream of an eagle,

Dark, moisture-laden clouds suppress the heights of Glencoe, whilst areas of blue sky and sunshine accentuate the contrast between the tremendous primeval energy of the coldly gleaming torrent and the striking irregularity of the terraces over which the great cascade

down. On either side of the strath rise mountains which have a singular, dark beauty all their own – composed of rocks thousands of millions of years old, and called 'metamorphic' because in the course of their torturous history they have been violently

Above: Eilean Donnan Castle on its island promontory overlooking the steel-grey waters of Loch Duich.

'Hill-tops like hot iron glitter bright in the sun,
And the rivers we're eying burn to gold as they run;
Burning hot is the ground, liquid gold is the air;
Whoever looks round sees Eternity there.'

The burnished gold of sunset reflects upon Loch
Garry *above;* Loch Creran in Argyllshire *right* and
Glenfinnan at the head of Loch Sheil *left.* The latter's
sense of timelessness, and depth of history associated
with the area, is heightened by the statue of Prince
Charlie, commemorating the raising of the Jacobite
Standard on the spot in 1745. Indeed, there is always a
sough of the 'forty-five' among the pines and larches a
Glenfinnan, and a sob and a heartache in the wind
whispering through them. Here the scent of resinous fi
needles mingles with that of bog-myrtle, and no-one
comes by this monument without seeing in their mind's
eye the galleys of the Highland clans sailing up Loch
Sheil to the mustering ground of 1745.

The herring port of Mallaig *above* on the rocky shore of North Morar is
the western end of the balladeer's 'Road to the Isles', and its neighbouring
waters are among the deepest and darkest in Britain. Loch Morar, a few
miles south, is more than 1,000 ft deep and is said to possess a monster
which appears whenever a death is imminent in the clan MacDonald.

The Caledonian Canal (seen *right*, at Corpach) is a magnificent relic of
19th-century engineering, which took 44 years to complete, and when it was opened
in 1847 was regarded as a wonder of the age – providing sheltered passage
between the Irish and North Seas. The canal runs the length of the fissure of the
Great Glen, and is an impressive monument to Telford, its designer.

The Orkneys – remote isles of treeless moor and rugged cliffs (*below,* at Cruden Bay) – have a long history of settlement which predate their medieval ownership by Denmark, Norway and – since 1496 – Scotland, by thousands of years. Excavations have revealed dwellings used by a Neolithic people who were the contemporaries of the builders of the Stone Age monuments in Southern England – the most notable of which have come to light at Skara Brae *lower left and right,* a site once engulfed in a sea of sand, but then uncovered afresh by a storm. Brochs dating from the Pictish Era have also been excavated at Gurness Earthworks *opposite page.*

The famous Cross of Lorraine *above* on Lyle Hill, Greenock was erected to honour those Free French who died in the Atlantic. *Right:* amid a wild landscape – the haunt of wildcats and badgers, crossbills, sparrow hawks and golden eagles – stands the ruined husk of Kilchurn Castle, romantically sited on a spit of land jutting into Loch Awe. Kilchurn Castle moved Wordsworth to write of it – 'Child of loud-throated War! the mountain-stream roars in thy hearing; but thy hour of rest is come, and thou art silent in thy age.'

From the placid waters of a lake run the bracken and heath covered slopes of the Glencoe massif *right*, rising into the wave-like mountainous buttress originally hewn by ice, and now shining under a light scattering of snow. Its form recalls to mind Stephenson's words '... where the old red hills are bird-enchanted, and the low green meadows bright with sward'.

Ragged layers of cinereous cloud hang over the grey water of Loch Achnacarry *left*, and dark shadows fall upon the heights of Ben Lui *below left* by the little village of Tyndrum. On the shore of Loch Fyne is Inverary Castle *below*, the heraldic seat of the Dukes of Argyll, and the headquarters of the clan Campbell since the early 15th century.

Glenfinnan, a magnificent site at the entrance to three glens, was
chosen as the mustering ground of the clans during the 1745 Jacobite
rising. The Camerons and the MacDonalds gathered to the standard, as
did some Stewarts and Rob Roy's MacGregors. Here – where now stands
the clan memorial *above* – James was proclaimed King of Great Britain
and Ireland, and his commission was read out appointing 'our dearest

son Charles, Prince of Wales, to be our sole regent in our Kingdoms'.
After much glory, much mismanagement, and with success almost achieved,
the campaign eventually foundered in disaster at Culloden moor.
Inverlochy Castle *left*, beneath the intimidating shadow of Ben
Nevis, retains the ancient name of the nearby town rechristened
'Fort William' after the first Scottish rising of 1715.

The water-meads of Scotland,
half-veiled in sun-shot mist;
Renfrewshire *facing page.*

If the building of fortified tower-houses bears a direct relationship to the prevailing level of violence and disorder then there is no better breeding ground than the medieval realm of Scotland. The wealth of such castles (Eilean Donnan and Castle Stalker on Loch Laich, *below and below right,* being prime examples) is evident throughout the land; and bears silent witness to the remark made in 1498 by Don Pedro de Ayala that 'the Scots spend all their time in wars, and when there is no war they fight one another.' These bastions are quiet places now, that seem to belong to their past, half asleep in the shadows of their castle keeps.

Eilean Donnan castle *above right,* built on a tiny, rocky island by Alexander II in 1220 to combat Viking raiders, was bombarded into submission by the English warship 'Worcester' during the Jacobite rebellion when it was occupied by Spanish mercenaries. The castle was later rebuilt from rubble by clan MacRae.

Wide flush the fields; the softening air is balm;
Echo the mountain round; the forest smiles . . .
Where, o'er the rock, the scarcely waving pine
Fills the brown shade with a religious awe'

Silver birch and oaks – mellowing to the pale gold of
autumn – lie in the strath *right* and are highlighted
against the dark shadow of conifer forests as the
ascending land gains the brae of Balquhidder

Above: a highland pasture
wrested from the forest

There is a language wrote on earth and sky
By God's own pen in silent majesty:
There is a voice that's heard and felt and seen
In spring's young shades and summer's endless green.

Into the beauty of the Scottish landscape Clare's verse steals effortlessly. The gentle breath of summer touches the shore of Loch Tummel *right* and Loch Eil *below and bottom left*, and brings to the River Coe *left* and Sgurr Fhuaran *bottom* a sense of calm and abiding serenity.

Nature has wrought scenery of unparalleled spectacle in the Highlands, yet lying within this wild region are glimpses of a landscape of milder shade: for here, among the airy ridges and leaping torrents, are rolling sheep pastures *lower right* set here and there with lonely tarns or trenched with shallow burns. Here also are found deer forests embracing both woods and high grazing for cattle and horses (as seen at Strath Mashie, *right*). For winter feeding hay is harvested, and the crop is usually gathered by machine *lower left*, but the further north one travels, the more the likelihood that traditional methods of hand gathering into stooks prevail. The crofters at Colla Firth *above left* use just such a method – erecting conical haystacks for drying – a practice that has been handed down throughout the centuries.

The delicate woodland flower, the Star of Bethlehem *above*, braves the cold of April and May to open its wan, milk-white petals amid the rank growth of ivy and fern.

Evening by the shoreline of Loch Eil *above* wherein the pale gold and grey of the sky finds faithful echo in the unstirred waters of the 'linn'. As the light fails, a ghostly mist rises from the heart of the silent lake. At Whiteness Voe *right*

colour is fast fading from the landscape, soon to be engulfed in a monochromatic infinity. The limitless, enigmatic character of this land of sea, loch and mountain, beneath a vast open sky, is most potent, most poignant, in the pause of the hour after dusk.

Raised within settings of unequalled splendour, the ancient castles of the Highlands guard the routeways of gleaming loch and fern-rusted glen. Eilean Donnan *below, left and bottom left* stands sentinel at the strategic confluence of Lochs Duich, Alsh and Long whilst Urquhart Castle *facing page and bottom right* rises 50 ft above the monster-haunted waters of Loch Ness, to control movement along the Great Glen – the pass out of the Western Highlands along which clan MacDonald, the Lords of the Isles, travelled in

search of plunder. Thus was raised (upon the site of a Norman motte, and an even earlier Iron Age hillfort) a 13th century stone castle, built 'for a defence against the attacks of robbers and malefactors.'

and of quiet and pensive grace whose variety is infinite. Scotland woos
the eye with the beauty of its green solitude; of secluded lochs of silver
streams singing among moors (of heather-honey taste upon each name),
of winding sheeptracks, of lonely castle ruins *left*, whose crumbling

stones speak of past wars, of past forays – and of douce grey fishing hamlets
above sheltered in the lee of brooding peaks which rear their craggy tops –
a soft blue when the sun shines upon them, or gloomy and threatening when
the wind hunts the darkling storm clouds across their desolate summits.

Fishing boats and pleasure steamers are the main users of the lochs and waterways; and it is here – where mountains slope down to the lakeside margins – that the awesome majesty of Highland scenery may at times be 'softened' by the occasional glimpse of a cottage or croft. The paddle steamer 'Waverley' *bottom left* is viewed in the Kyles of Bute; and yachts are at anchor on Loch Leven *left* and on the Crinan canal *bottom* which connects Loch Fyne and the Firth of Clyde with the Western Isles. Further north, at Fort William, the 500 million year old granite mass of Ben Nevis reflects in the chill waters of Loch Linnhe *below*.

Ranged along the sheltered inlet of Loch Carron is the fishing hamlet of Plockton *facing page*, flanked on the north by the Applecross mountains, which appear to rise like spectres from the turquoise calm of Loch Torridon.

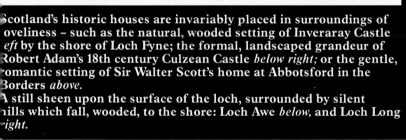

Scotland's historic houses are invariably placed in surroundings of loveliness – such as the natural, wooded setting of Inveraray Castle *left* by the shore of Loch Fyne; the formal, landscaped grandeur of Robert Adam's 18th century Culzean Castle *below right;* or the gentle, romantic setting of Sir Walter Scott's home at Abbotsford in the Borders *above.*

A still sheen upon the surface of the loch, surrounded by silent hills which fall, wooded, to the shore: Loch Awe *below,* and Loch Long *right.*

The Scottish Lowlands, rather than the border country, were the
cockpit of fighting between the English and the Scots for hundreds of
years. Stirling *left*, the 'Gateway to the Highlands', on the fringe
of the Lowland belt, witnessed some of the fiercest engagements. Its
moment of greatest triumph occurred in 1314 when, at the famous

battlefield at Bannockburn, Bruce defeated a vastly superior English
force under the command of Edward II.
Above, the snow-covered heights, crags and corries of Ben Vorlich
become less ice-bound as they slope to the crystal, shimmering waters
of Loch Earn.

Above at Glen Etive the thoughts of Wordsworth seem to carry in the frozen, still air: '. . . a silver current flows, with uncontrolled meanderings'.

Scotland's mountain landscape is one of foreboding crags, rigs and moors, marked here and there with a fan of scree thrown out by

glacial cries of the distant past. It seems a cold and lonely place, snow-laden for much of the year and often assailed by driving rain; yet beauty, when it is to be found – perhaps in the play of cloud-shadows on the frozen slopes, or the trail of mist across the rocky faces of mountains – is, by its unsuspected nature, all the

Right **Loch Morlich and the Cairngorms**

Loch Ness *below and left* is one of a chain of lochs lying in the Great Glen, and extends from Inverness *right* – popularly dubbed 'the Capital of the Highlands' – to Fort Augustus. Its waters are darkened by peaty soil brought down to the loch by the numerous small streams and rivers that feed it. The murky depths are supposedly the haunt of its famous monster – stories of which stretch back to the 6th century (when St Columba prevented it from eating a Pict) and beyond, into the mists of Gaelic lore, which states that an 'each Visque', or 'fearsome water-horse', inhabits every dark sheet of water in the Highlands.

Above Castle Urquhart, sited on an elevated spit of land jutting out into Loch Ness.

'By Tummel and Loch Rannoch and Lochaber I will go,
by heather-hills with heaven in their wiles . . .'

Loch Rannoch *left* is lovely, but Loch Tummel is lovelier still. High
above its waters you can stand upon a little wooded eminence and see

the view which Queen Victoria so often delighted to look upon: richly
wooded slopes, purple hills melting into blue sky, and the still
sheen on the bosom of the loch.

Like their Viking forefathers, the inhabitants of the Orkneys and Shetlands are tied to the sea, and many picturesque harbours dot the islands – Stromness *below left*, St Margaret's Hope *right*, and Scalloway *left and below.*
Above Cantick Head lighthouse, overlooking the Pentland Firth.

The most notable physical feature of Edinburgh is its 822 foot high 'mountain in miniature' – Arthur's Seat which, together with the Salisbury Crags on its lower slopes, rises almost directly above Holyroodhouse *right* to command impressive views over the capital *left* and beyond. Some twenty miles to the east is the famous light of the Bass Rock *above*.
The statue of Allan Ramsay *below right* in Princes Street Gardens.

Above, the greens and golds of an Orkney spring – at Finstown on the Bay of Firth.

The frieze of mountains that encircles Loch Leven *right* takes on a wistful, cerulean blue, lying in the shadow of day's dawning. These awesome ranges share the landscape with icy streams that tumble through green and wooded glens – with frowning crags and darkened passes, with the calm waters of the vast inland loch and, above all else, with the ever-changing sky that gives rise to an immense variety of shade and subtle colouring.

Glasgow *these pages* is the largest city and seaport in Scotland. It has grown with enormous rapidity within the last 150 years, due largely to the enterprise of Glaswegians in developing the River Clyde *left, below left and above*. Today, the traditional shipbuilding of the area is augmented by the construction of oil and gas rigs *below centre. Right* Glasgow's Kelvingrove Park, and *below* the statue of Sir Walter Scott which dominates George Square.

These pages: the City of Dundee rises augustly beside the Firth of Tay, which is crossed by the graceful, two-mile-long Tay Railway Bridge of 1887 and, eighty years its junior, the new road bridge linking Dundee with Fife and the South.

Rich in turrets and gables, the Scottish Baronial style is exemplified by Crathes Castle *below,* and Balmoral Castle *above, right and below left* – the Royal Estate which encompasses a chateau-like castle (the fantasy of the Prince Consort), green farm land, formal gardens, heather moors and sombre expanses of deer forest.

Left, the Royal Burgh of Montrose, sited on the estuary of the South Esk River.

The Royal Burgh of Aberdeen *these pages* lies on the estuaries of the rivers Dee and Don, and is built almost entirely of local granite. It is the third largest city in Scotland, and the country's largest fishing port. In recent years the traditional trawling boats *left* have had to share the harbour with an ever-increasing flotilla of larger shipping *above* supplying offshore oil rigs; such are their numbers that Aberdeen is now of outstanding importance as the North Sea oil capital.

The soul of the Highlands lies in the mist-capped mountain heights
above the ordinary haunts of men. The very names of some of them
have a quality of godlike mystery and grandeur, even of terror –
Stobinian, Lochnagar and dark Schiehallion. The latter *left* rises

for 3,547 feet above Loch Rannoch, and is one of the best known
landmarks in the Central Highlands.
Gleneagles Hotel *above*, the famous golf resort, lies on moorland near
the village of Auchterarder, between Strath Allan and Strath Earn.

Nature has given her beauty to the waters and mountains; and the silent, still loch shimmers with the fading silver light of evening. At such times the shadowed hills assert new dominance – as at Blaven on the Isle of Skye *above* – and the ruined husks of Scotland's ancient castles *right* brood heavily upon the scene, as though laden down by the weight of the centuries.

'Edina! Scotia's darling seat! All hail thy palaces and tow'rs . . . There Architecture's noble pride Bids elegance and splendour rise'.

Burns knew the beautiful city of Edinburgh well; and he is one of many poets and ballad-writers urged to praise the Scottish capital – a city through the streets of which innumerable writers have followed the history of an ancient and romantic Kingdom; a city along whose flagstones, wynds and closes pass the ghosts of Kings and Queens, and of the illustrious who have done so much to make Scotland great.

Left, Edinburgh's Royal Mile. *Below left*, the castle and Arthur's Seat (also *opposite page*). *Below*, the city centre from the castle battlements and *right* Charlotte Square and Calton Hill.

There are few beauties to compare with that of a Highland loch, hemmed in by immemorial hills. Sunlight glints on the water, which is as clear as a mirror – save where the mountain shadow falls darkly across it.

roll down to the lake's edge, and over all, silence and tranquility lie like a mantle of peace.
Above Loch Moy in Inverness, and *right* Loch Shiel in the Western

The 'Golden Fringes of Fife' run right round the coastline of the Ness – a ribbon of blue sea and yellow sand, intermittently punctuated by charming fishing villages, such as Crail *above left*, Anstruther *far left* and St Monance *above*. On the northern shores of Fife Ness stands the Royal Burgh of St Andrews *right,* which for many people spells nothing but golf – for its incomparable links makes it the Mecca of the 'Royal and Ancient Game St Andrews, however, is also the spiritual centre of Scotland (even though its cathedral now lies in ruins) and boasts the oldest university in the country. Some 15 miles inland is another Royal Burgh, that of Falkland *left,* whose ancient palace was a favoured seat of the Scottish Court.

The River Dochart *these pages* is typical of many Highland rivers which have their birth in the peat moors of distant hills – whose silver dazzle and splash becomes a raging torrent of exploding white water

lifting and leaping out from the rocks – a form without fetter or shape. The deep-voiced rush of sound drowns all else, and a fine, cold vapour perpetually drifts across dripping stone.

'The mountains against heaven's grave weight
Rise up, and grow to wonderous height'
In summer months the softer, more poetic light of a moister, warmer climate informs scenes of picturesque splendour with a strange and irrepressible charm. Here are found the main elements – mountains, lochs and islands – in the triumph of Highland beauty. *Left* Loch Leven and the Glenduror Heights; *below* the 'Three Sisters' of Glencoe; and the Lochan Fada *right*.

Perhaps the most picturesque of all the islands lying off the Scottish mainland, the 'Isle of Mist' – Skye *these pages* – is the largest of the Inner Hebrides. The Isle of Skye is famous for its range of jagged black mountains, known as the Cuillins, and its coast is endlessly indented by the sea. Fishing harbours abound – Kyleakin *above and right*, and Portree *left* – being notable examples. Inland stands Dunvegan Castle *below*, and the tiny crofting community of Tarskavaig *above left*.

Lying by the lochside, the crofting and fishing villages of Shieldaig *below left*, and Plockton *left* are sheltered in the lee of distant stone craigs. Plockton is beautifully sited on a small inlet of Loch Carron *below*.
Right, Loch Arkaig; and *above* the winter ski-slopes at Aviemore.

Right, the 'Fair City' of Perth on the Tay River. Some 15 miles to the west is the village of Crieff *left* where stands Drummond Castle *above left*, once bombarded by Cromwell. *Below*, Arbroath Harbour and, *above* springtide flowers beside the sparkling burn at Aberfeldy.

The diffused light of the Highlands plays amazing tricks of colour – whether in the violet shades of evening at Loch Linnhe *right*, or the fiery tones of sunset over Loch Eil *above*. The latter is contrasted with the pale lilac of dawn upon the lake *left*, where the schooner 'Captain Scott' lies at anchor in veils of mist *below*.

The Caledonian Canal *below and below left*; and the Glenfinnan viaduct *left* seem to have become almost a part of the landscape.

Above Oban Harbour, and *right* Ben Nevis from Loch Linnhe, with Fort William on the far shore.

It does not take any upland byway long to rise out of its glen to the high country of the mountains – through woods that degenerate into clumps of birch and hazel growing on land that hardens with every hundred feet of altitude gained, until there is only bare rock and moorland scrub. It is not a comfortable scene that meets the wayfarer's eye – but one to marvel at in all its gaunt and threatening majesty.

Above Glen Shee. *Opposite page*, Loch Tay.

Sited between St Monance and Anstruther on the Fife coast, the Royal Burgh of Pittenweem *these pages* compounds a delightful scene of old red houses grouped around its ancient fishing harbour. Nearby is the cave-shrine of St Fillan; and some 40 miles westward along the shore of the Firth is Culross – associated with both St Kentigern and St Serf. The town nestles in Torry Bay, and well justifies its reputation as the loveliest of the old Fife Burghs – having the supreme benefit of being under the control of the Scottish National Trust, who have admirably preserved many old buildings – among which are some typical 17th century houses *above* with crow-stepped gables and red painted roofs.

Cawdor Castle in the Highlands *left* is one of the finest and best preserved of Scotland's medieval buildings. Shakespeare's Macbeth was Thane of Cawdor, and the castle is traditionally associated with Duncan's murder. Another ancient seat is Blair Castle in the Central Highlands *above*. The 'Baronial style' is echoed at Dunbeath Castle in Caithness *above left*.
Right the Glenfinnan Viaduct skirts the shoreline of Loch Shiel; and *above right* Loch Lochy forms one of a chain of lochs in the Great Glen.

Edinburgh Castle *above*, perched on a great mass of volcanic rock, overlooks Princes Street, the Old Town and the distant Firth. The citadel so crowns the promontory that it is precipitous on three sides, and was so well defended on the fourth that, throughout the centuries of medieval warfare with the English its summit remained inaccessible to attacking forces – save for two occasions: in 1296 when it fell to King Edward I, and 45 years later, when it was recaptured by the Scots.

Right The Royal Mile separates the castle stronghold from the sovereign's 16th century Palace of Holyrood.

The two great bridges of the Forth – the modern road bridge *above*, and the Victorian railway bridge *right*. The latter is one of the finest examples of engineering in the world, and has a total length of 2,765 yards including the approach viaducts. It crosses the Firth giving a headway of 150 feet, the two main spans each having dimensions of 1,710 feet.

The road and rail bridge at Connel in Strathclyde *overleaf* spans the mouth of Loch Etive, with the Falls of Lora below. It is the largest cantilever bridge in Europe after the Forth Bridge.